# Saint Juan Diego

# Saint Juan Diego
*And Our Lady of Guadalupe*

Written by
**Josephine Nobisso**

Illustrated by
**Virginia Esquinaldo**

**Pauline**
BOOKS & MEDIA

Boston

Library of Congress Cataloging-in-Publication Data

Nobisso, Josephine.
    Saint Juan Diego and our Lady of Guadalupe / written
by    Josephine Nobisso ; illustrated by Virginia Esquinaldo.
        p. cm.
    ISBN 0-8198-7064-1 (pbk.)
    1. Juan Diego, Saint, ca. 1474–1548. 2. Guadalupe, Our
Lady    of. I. Esquinaldo, Virginia. II. Title.
    BX4700.J76 N63 2002
    232.91.'7'097253—dc21

                                                    2002005836

"P" and Pauline are registered trademarks of the Daughters of St. Paul.

Text copyright © 2002, Josephine Nobisso

Edition copyright © 2002, Daughters of St. Paul

Published by Pauline Books & Media, 50 Saint Pauls Avenue, Boston,
MA 02130-3491. www.pauline.org

Printed in the U.S.A.

SJD VSAUSAPEOILL2-610084 7064-1

Pauline Books & Media is the publishing house of the Daughters of
St. Paul, an international congregation of women religious serving
the Church with the communications media.

6  7  8  9  10                              21  20  19  18  17

*For even more titles in the*
*Encounter the Saints series,*
*visit: www.pauline.org./EncountertheSaints*

# Contents

## 1

# BACK FROM THE DEAD

No one knew that when they buried Princess Papantzin she was still alive. Suddenly, the quiet of the lush palace gardens was shattered by her screams from within the damp tomb. Hummingbirds scattered, and spotted leopards yowled in fear. Members of the royal household, who had been mourning her death, came running. "Unseal the tomb!" they cried, their faces ashen with terror.

Princess Papantzin stumbled out, skin tingling from the effects of the strange dream she had had while in her coma. "Alert my brother!" she ordered.

Emperor Montezuma II listened wide-eyed as his sister described her experience. "My vision was a prophecy meant for you!" she exclaimed. "In my dream I met a man all made of light. He wore a kind of symbol on his forehead—two intersecting black lines. I followed him to the edge of the great sea.

We stared into the mists over the water. Suddenly, the fog parted and I gasped at vast canoes that loomed over me, bounding toward the shore.

"The vessels were carrying men from a faraway land—men who are our people's long-awaited messengers from the god, *Quetzalcoatl* (KETS-ahl-KO-waht). They are the prophesied foreigners who will conquer you, Montezuma. They will finally bring knowledge of the true God to our people, the Aztecs."

"I have expected this," the emperor murmured. "How shall I know when all you saw is about to be fulfilled?"

"The billowing white sails of the vessels also bore the symbol of the intersecting lines," Princess Papantzin told her brother. "It was as if that symbol itself were the force that drew the great canoes to Mexico's shores."

"The symbol?" Emperor Montezuma asked. The Mexican tribes already honored a symbol made of two intersecting lines. The vertical line stood for things that descended from the supernatural world, and the horizontal line stood for earthly things.

At the point where the two lines touched—the center of this "cross"—the Aztecs believed that the worlds of heaven and earth met. "So," the emperor reasoned, "it is to be by this sign that our empire will fall and the Aztecs will be given a new life!"

# 2
# GOD'S GREAT PLAN

Princess Papantzin, who had fallen into a coma, was accidentally buried alive in 1505. That was thirteen years after Christopher Columbus had landed in another part of the New World. At that time, the Aztecs of ancient Mexico were still waiting to learn whether any of the many gods they worshipped was the *true* one. "Perhaps," their priests told each other, "he will be a god we have failed to acknowledge!"

Another prophecy, based on the Aztec calendar, foretold: "The hour for gaining knowledge of the one true God will come soon. It will be a time that is both happy and sad, for that hour will also mark the end of our great Aztec culture." Although tremendous changes and upheavals were expected, Emperor Montezuma and the Aztecs looked forward to them. "If a nation becomes friends with the one true God," they told each other, "it can petition him for all its needs. It will then have security, and its people can live in peace."

Along with their many shrines dedicated to the gods of nature, the Aztecs had erected a great shrine reserved for the true God whom they did not yet know. They called him "the God through whom everything lives." But on the pedestal of that vacant temple, no figure or graven image had ever been placed. "No one knows whom to honor there," the Aztecs said when they passed it.

Princess Papantzin's dream encouraged her brother Montezuma. He had to wait another fourteen years, however, before the prophesied strangers appeared. In 1519, when the thirty-four-year-old Spanish explorer Hernando Cortes landed in what is now Mexico with his band of about 650 Spaniards and a handful of Indians, a rumor reached Montezuma: the Europeans' helmets were decorated with a cross!

"Bring me one of these helmets!" Montezuma commanded. Sure enough, there on its front, was a cross—the very sign his sister had seen in her dream.

God was preparing the moment that would shape the history not only of the "new" land, called the "Americas," but also of the "old" world in Europe.

"The Church is suffering," Catholic Europeans said. "Because of some scandals and the heresies being spread among the people, millions have lost the faith. Now some are thinking that they can reform the Church on their own."

Other Catholics reminded each other, "We need to remember that no matter what happens, it is Jesus, God himself, who always leads and cares for his Church. Jesus never abandons us!"

Another issue dividing Christians in Europe at this time was the use of holy objects. Down through the centuries many people had found that focusing their attention on a holy object helped them to pray. For example, the Israelites had the Ark of the Covenant and the scroll of God's Law. Catholics later used holy pictures or statues to remind them of Jesus, the Blessed Virgin and the saints as they prayed. But some European Christians were now insisting that holy objects no longer be used. This only added to the growing disagreement between different groups of people.

God was about to restore the faith of his people in Europe, the Old World, by a miracle that would take place for his people in the New World. He would reveal his covenant to this other portion of his people, the native peoples of the New World, who had not yet heard the Gospel. Just as he had used Mary's help to bring Jesus into the world, God would now use her to bring Jesus to many who had never heard of him. In a short while, God would send the Mother of his Son to Mexico....

Perhaps God even gave a hint of the wonderful miracle yet to come. During the Age of Exploration, ships destined to carry the sons and daughters of Europe on dangerous journeys were crafted with extreme care. Great thought was also given to the selection of their names. Most ships were placed under the patronage of favorite saints. The crew would ask the patron saint of the ship to intercede with God for a safe voyage.

Leaving Europe to sail into the unknown, Christopher Columbus (whose first name means "Christ-bearer") was given three ships for his voyage across the Atlantic Ocean. All three were christened in honor of the Blessed Mother: *La Niña*, *La Pinta* and *La Santa Maria*. *La Santa Maria* was Columbus's main or flag ship.

Columbus reached land in 1492. This was only thirty-nine years before Mary appeared to a native man named Juan Diego in Mexico. Columbus went ashore with what appeared to be a promise and a prophecy that God would "paint" the image of his young Mother for his people. Read together as *La Pinta Niña Santa Maria*, the names of Columbus's three ships translate to: *The painted girl, Holy Mary.*

*"God loves us more than we can imagine."*

## 3

## SERIOUS TROUBLES

The Mexica, native peoples of the land we now call Mexico, were curious about the Spaniards' cross. The Indians used a written language not of letters, as we know them. Theirs was a complex system of drawings, different from, but comparable to the hieroglyphics of Egypt. Instead of letters, they drew figures, or pictographs, which looked very much like what they represented.

The twelve Franciscan friars who arrived in the New World in 1524 were on fire with love for Jesus and for his Church. The great dream of these missionaries was to spread the Gospel. Using things the Indians could see and touch, such as holy pictures and statues, the friars enthusiastically explained all the wonderful things God had done for the human race. "God loves us more than we can imagine," they said as they showed the people the crucifix with its image of Jesus' body nailed to it. "He sent his own Son to be one of us and to die so that we could live with God someday."

Many of the native people not only embraced the Spaniards' God, whom they understood to be the "one" and "true" God, they also experienced a great sense of relief and freedom. "The doctrine of this God makes sense!" they exclaimed.

"For as long as we can remember," the converts explained to the friars, "we have worshipped many gods: the sun god, the moon god, the star god. We feared the fierce and greedy goddess, *Tonantzin* (toh-NAN-seen), the 'mother' goddess who 'lives' on Tepeyac Hill, and who was never satisfied, no matter how much blood of our children the Aztecs offered her.

"We believed that the gods changed, as nature changes. They brought good weather or they made storms. They parched the land or they hid the sun. They made the earth quake and they spewed out terrifying lava. To us, this universe of gods seemed always on the edge of disaster. It had to be held in constant balance. 'The gods must be angry!' we cried whenever troubles came!"

The friars told them, "You were not alone in these beliefs. The people of the Old Testament believed that *someone* must certainly be above humans. Ancient people were aware that events often happened independent of the will of man. Some 'being,' they reasoned, or perhaps *many* beings, were greater than humans."

"Yes! That's it!" the Indian converts exclaimed. "And we wanted to honor and worship this greater intelligence."

The friars understood. "And since you saw God's work reflected in creation, it was easy to make gods and goddesses of the forces of nature," they reasoned.

"Yes," the native people went on. "And we offered them gifts that were gestures of our submission, petition, and thanksgiving. This showed that we depended on powers greater than our own."

"Your offerings were an effort to keep your gods happy," one of the Franciscans said kindly. "You hoped that in return for your worship, the gods would grant favors and blessings to your people."

"Of course!" one Indian man exclaimed. "The greater the gift, the more the gods would see that our people were serious about doing our part to keep the universe in balance."

The Indians explained to them that since, throughout the Americas, there were many tribes of people, many customs of worship had sprung up. The friars were able to point out that the same had been true in ancient Biblical times. "There were those who offered up the fruits of the harvest," the missionaries told the people. "And there were those who sacrificed the blood of animals. There were those who performed personal penances and those who imposed them on others."

"However," the Mexica explained, "our neighbors, the Aztecs, have fallen into a horrible practice! They believe that human life is the most valuable thing on earth and that blood is the most precious liquid. And they are right. But because of this, the Aztecs also think that they will get the best treatment from the gods if they offer them human sacrifices and blood. They even believe that if they don't give blood to the sun god, the sun will stop shining and the world will come to an end! They are really convinced that it is their duty to make these offerings to their gods."

The friars understood the situation. "Abraham was once about to sacrifice his own son," they told the Indians, "but an angel of the Lord stopped him. Instead, God sent his own Son as the perfect sacrifice, the one sacrifice that ends all others. If only your neighbors knew what a terrible mistake they're making!"

The Indians spelled out the problem that Mexico was having. "The Aztec name for 'blood,' is 'flowers.' This is why the Aztec tribe calls their terrible raids on our villages the 'Flower Wars.' They kidnap our children and adults. They make these victims their slaves for a time, or they immediately drag the prisoners away into temples where they are sacrificed to the gods. Since one sacrifice does not always obtain the protection and favor of the gods, the Aztecs kill large numbers of our people!"

"All that blood shed in vain to please gods that don't even exist!" the Franciscans cried.

"Even the ball games," one of the Indians went on, "the *tlachtli* (TLACH-tlee), in the great stadium, are played to please the gods. The price for losing the game? Death."

"Sometimes," another added, "the price for winning is also death!"

"I see," one of the priests said. "The most valuable player makes the most valuable sacrifice to the gods."

A leader of the native people spoke up. "We, all the tribes with whom the Aztecs have been warring, want to end these troubles, but the Flower Wars have been getting worse and worse. A neighboring tribe, the Tlaxcalans, is now threatening war in defense of the captives."

As the years passed, Bishop Juan Zumarraga, who was also a Franciscan, often pondered the situation. The struggle was growing so fierce, and the resentment toward the ruling Aztecs so intense that nothing short of a miracle would bring peace to the New World and free it from the horror of human sacrifice.

In his palace, Montezuma, too, was pondering. Even though the message from Papantzin's angelic companion predicted the Aztecs' defeat, the emperor rejoiced. *The true God will soon be revealed!* he reminded himself. Montezuma and his people had always yearned to praise the one God they could call "true." But what sort of sacrifice would this God require?

Montezuma wondered.

## 4

# THE GOOD NEWS

Among the native people who eagerly embraced the new Christian religion were three Chichimeca Indians, Cuauhtlotzin, his wife Malitzin, and his uncle. All three were baptized, receiving the new names Juan Diego, Maria Lucia and Juan Bernardino.

"God does not want human sacrifice," the friars explained to the people. "The Aztec priests sacrifice blood that is not their own. Instead, the one true God became a man and offered his own blood to save the people he himself had created. No amount of stolen blood could ever equal one drop of the blood of the God of Life!"

The oppressed Indians, loving and gentle, also understood and responded to the idea of God sending his Son to bring salvation to the world. "If an Indian child cries," they told the friars, "the person closest to him comforts him, even if that person is not the child's relative. We show love and affection to all our children."

Because they were especially kind and caring toward their children, the Indians understood that the true God, who had willed to sacrifice his only Son for humanity, must love the human race very much. They said, "God has given us Jesus, his precious Son, the most innocent, in fact, of all innocent children."

The Indians also placed great importance on the good of the whole community. "The tribe," they said, "and not the individual, is at the center of things." They practiced courtesy toward each other. It seemed reasonable, then, that the one true God, the Father of all, would never wish them to harm each other. "God is certainly displeased with human sacrifice!" they concluded.

Since the personal needs of each Indian were subjected to the needs of the group, and decisions were made in common, every person was responsible for the well being of the other, especially of children, whose needs were greater. To the Mexica, who had practiced self-sacrifice for the welfare of others, the idea of God having sacrificed himself for all people made perfect sense. It proved his perfect love.

The most difficult god to please, and the least understandable of all the Aztec gods (even to the Aztecs themselves) was the feathered-serpent *Quetzalcoatl* (KETS-ahl-KO-waht). "His ways are very mysterious," those Aztecs who came for Christian instruction explained. "He is the warrior god. Our ancient prophecies say that he will rescue the human world from the dark underworld—not through war and sacrificing others' blood, but through personal sacrifice! He is the hero of our civilization. He will make us great!"

The Aztecs themselves didn't understand how this god, who was to preserve their culture, could also be a warrior who would first change their culture. Montezuma and his people knew the date of Quetzalcoatl's prophesied return. "His return will coincide with the fall of our empire," Montezuma's advisors said. The emperor realized that the arrival of the Spanish colonists and the revelation of God fulfilled the ancient prophecies, sealing the Aztecs' destiny.

The Spanish priests, in the meantime, were teaching how, in the Mass, Jesus offers himself as a perfect sacrifice to God the Father for the salvation of all people. "The Mass is our greatest prayer of adoration, contrition, thanksgiving and petition," they taught the people. "It is both a sacrifice and a holy meal. When we receive Communion, we are receiving the body, blood, soul and divinity of God's own Son, Jesus Christ. The one true God governs everything. The Mass brings God's infinitely strong assistance to us. We worship God and acknowledge his power. We love God because he is all good and deserves our love."

Belief in their most powerful god, the feathered-serpent Quetzalcoatl, had prepared the Aztecs to embrace the true God. It provided the seed of the Gospel—a seed that burst into bloom with the teachings of the Franciscans.

"The cross," the friars taught the Indians, "was once a symbol of disgrace. But since Jesus died on the cross out of love for us, sacrificing his life to save us from our sins, the cross has been changed into a symbol of honor. Our God changes things around. Our God brings us freedom. The cross is a symbol of these things."

The connection between the Franciscans —the Friars of the Immaculate Conception, consecrated to Mary—and converts like Juan Diego, his wife, his uncle, and many other Indians was growing stronger. The time was almost ripe for the Blessed Mother to appear. And she chose to appear to Juan Diego. Perhaps she chose Juan because of his simple love for God. Perhaps it was because of his humble position in the New World, which was now populated with learned and powerful men from both the Indian and European cultures.

Although we don't know very much about Juan Diego's origins, we do know that he probably belonged to the lower middle class. It's generally believed that he was born in 1474, in the village of *Cuautitlan* (KWAU-tee-TLAN), just outside the gates of Mexico City.

Juan seems to have been a farmer who owned a small plot of land he had inherited from his father. Besides working in the fields, Juan supported himself and his family by weaving mats out of the reeds that grew along the shores of Lake Texcoco.

Juan Diego's Aztec name was *Cuauh-tlotatzin* (KWAU-tloh-TA-tzin), which means, "the one who speaks like a eagle." Mary, the Mother of God, would soon use Juan's voice to focus everyone's attention on Jesus—her Son and her God.

# 5

# ENTER THE SPANIARDS

Adventurers all, Hernando Cortes and his men were delighted and surprised at the strangeness and richness of the culture they encountered in Mexico. The Aztecs had not been the first settlers there, but they had become the most powerful. They eventually ruled over the descendants of both the Mayan and Toltec tribes, blending many of the traditions and skills of these tribes with their own.

Emperor Montezuma lived in a great city called *Tenochtitlan* (teh-NOACH-tee-TLAN) which, according to Aztec legend, was the center of the world. His tribe had wandered through the land looking for the holy spot that their god *Huitzilopochtli* (WEET-seel-oh-PAOCH-tli) had revealed to them. An eagle holding a serpent in its beak would mark this spot. This eagle would be perched on a pear cactus. One day, the wanderers saw just such an eagle sitting on a pear cactus on a swampy island in the middle of Lake Texcoco. They rejoiced and began building a huddled village of huts woven from the reeds they found growing there.

Soon, the Aztecs began filling in the swamp, following their neighbors' example of building square, rectangular or pyramid-shaped buildings of mud, adobe and bricks. Interestingly, none of the Indian tribes had yet discovered the vaulted arch, which had been making buildings of many shapes possible in Europe and other parts of the world for centuries. They did, however, plan their city in much the way other cultures had, with the important public buildings, such as temples and richly carved royal palaces, surrounding a vast central square.

The walls of the people's adobe houses were painted with whitewash to keep their interiors cool in the blistering sun. Canals and ditches criss-crossed the entire city to allow for drainage of the marshy land and the disposal of day-to-day wastes.

When one of the Spaniards, Bernal Diaz del Castillo, first laid eyes on Montezuma's city, he wrote, "Gazing on such wonderful sights, we did not know whether that which appeared before us was real, for on one side in the land there were great cities and in the lake, many more, and the lake itself was crowded with canoes, and on the causeway were many bridges at intervals, and in front of us stood the great City of the Mexicans."

As stunning as Tenochititlan appeared, all was not well within its confines. The inhabitants were having trouble getting clean water to drink. Aztec builders burned poisonous limestone to produce the whitewash paint. They dumped their debris into the waterways. Human waste from homes flowed, unprocessed, into the same water which was used for drinking, cooking and bathing. Blood from the pagan sacrifices flowed down the pyramid-shaped temples to seep into the water, further contaminating it.

The smoke of thousands of cooking fires hung over the humid valley, badly polluting the air. To add to the physical misery and the hatred from the neighboring tribes there was political unrest within the Aztec tribe itself: nobles and priests had been hatching plots to overthrow Emperor Montezuma.

Even so, in a very real sense, the Aztecs had indeed found the "center of the world" —the center of the New World, that is. If a map of the New World had existed at the time of Juan Diego, and had been folded to find its geographic center, the mark would have landed in the territory now known as Mexico. God had revealed his covenant to the ancient people of the Old Testament. He had promised that they would be his people and that he would be their God. God had not forgotten, however, the people of the New World. They, too, were his children. They, too, would learn about his plan, even if it were to be at a later date. Before he ascended into heaven, Jesus instructed his disciples to spread his Good News to the ends of the earth. To the explorers venturing across vast and deep uncharted waters, the New World must have seemed like just that.

Many of the Aztecs' religious rituals resembled the sacraments of Catholicism. The Indians practiced a form of baptism, initiated (confirmed) young people, performed marriage ceremonies, and held death rites. Their very concept of offering sacrifices to their gods echoed the Eucharistic sacrifice, the Mass, in which Jesus offers himself to the Father on our behalf.

As much as the Indians' rituals made them open to learning about the sacraments, they were only shadows, signs of things to come. Once the Indians, like Juan Diego, had experienced the grace that the true sacraments bring, they were willing to suffer anything to receive this grace. Juan Diego had to walk for hours just to attend catechism classes. Many other Indians had to face the opposition of their friends and families when they converted to Christianity.

Native prophecy would blend into Christian reality. God would stake a claim in the New World by sending his Mother to Tepeyac Hill to conquer the false mother goddess, Tonantzin.

Mary would bring the good news that had not yet been confirmed, but which the native peoples had always suspected. Through Mary's apparition to Juan Diego, these "ends of the earth" would become heaven's territory, too.

# 6

# A Prayer for Help

The more they learned of the God the Spaniards worshipped, the more the native converts loved him. The more they received the sacraments, the more their hearts became enflamed. Even though there were soon a number of devoted Indians, Bishop Juan Zumarraga had expected many more of the people to convert to Christianity. Unfortunately, two forces opposed the work of the Catholic missionaries. The first was the resistance of the Aztecs to this "new" religion. "They see it as destroying their power over other tribes," the bishop noted. And because he was a learned and compassionate man, Bishop Zumarraga understood the Aztecs' deeper motives. "They have become so dependent on their superstitious belief in gods that they truly believe there will be a catastrophe if these gods are not served."

Since many Aztecs and members of other tribes had become good friends with the Spaniards and were willing to fight against Montezuma, the emperor's warriors became even fiercer. "We refuse to hear about this God!" many protested. "We must continue to worship our gods who feel slighted now that some are adoring this 'God through whom everything lives!'"

The second force the bishop and the missionary priests faced was the evil of many of their own countrymen, the *conquistadors* or Spanish conquerors. While it was true that Cortes and his men wanted to see the spread of the Christian religion, they had other aims, too. "Spain's authority must be spread further into the world!" Cortes asserted. Under the command of the Spanish conqueror Diego Velasquez, Cortes had assisted in taking Cuba, where he had settled, marrying and building up a fortune through plantations and mines. He saw many further opportunities in Mexico. Even when Velasquez changed his mind about sending Cortes to explore Mexico, Cortes helped himself to ships and supplies and set sail with his men while Velasquez slept.

New explorers arrived in Mexico soon after Cortes first landed there. The greed of many of them equaled the zeal of the good friars. These conquistadors took advantage of the innocent and trusting nature of the Indians, either tricking or killing them for

*Some conquistadors killed the Indians for their gold.*

their gold. The Indians said, "Gold is good for ornamentation, but it has no money value. The shining dust that comes out of the earth crazes these foreigners! Gold is not even as valuable as dirt.... At least dirt has the power to grow things!"

The Spanish king had sent a delegation of men to oversee and govern his new colony. The cruel and unfair practices of these Spaniards saddened and outraged Bishop Zumarraga. He and his priests were becoming more and more frustrated in their attempts to spread the Good News of Jesus to the native peoples. "How can we, who practice the Catholic faith, convince the Indians about its truth and beauty if corrupt men profess to be followers of this same faith?" the bishop cried. And he was right.

Because of the foreigners who were evil, the Indians began to suspect all foreigners. It was becoming very hard for Bishop Zumarraga to win new friends for God and for God's universal Church. The situation even meant danger for his friars. The bishop needed a miracle as badly as the Indians needed one!

Bishop Zumarraga prayed for a sign. "Make it miraculous, not coincidental, Lord," he begged, "so that I may be sure of your holy will! The Castilian roses of my homeland do not grow here," he continued. "If you wish me to keep the missionaries here during this dangerous time, let some-one give me Spanish roses." Roses were also a symbol of Mary, the Immaculate Concep-tion, who was the patroness of his friars. "The choice of a rose shows that I desire that this sign come through your Mother's holy hands," Bishop Zumarraga prayed.

Because of the bishop's fervent prayer, and because the Aztecs used the symbol of flowers to signify blood, killing and sacri-fice, the sign that Mary would use was to have great meaning. She would use flowers not only to remove the bishop's fears, but also to reverse the Aztecs' thinking. She wanted to make it clear that her flowers did not signify the blood of death, but instead, the blood of her Son, Jesus, who is new Life for all people.

# 7

# AZTEC LIFE

Even though the Aztecs had been in the region only about 175 years, Emperor Montezuma's power extended over the vast territory of what is now Mexico. He exacted taxes, or tribute, from the other tribes. Tribute could be paid in the form of common products, many of them food. Since cows, horses, pigs, and sheep were not introduced into Aztec lands until the Spanish brought them, the native peoples ate the foods available in their area: frogs, lizards, turtles, fishes, and locusts. The Mexica raised rabbits and hairless dogs for eating, and collected snails, birds' eggs, honey and fish eggs. Green algae, skimmed from Lake Texcoco, was also part of their diet. The Indians paid tribute in mounds of cocoa pods ground into medicine, food, or a chocolate drink.

Much of the tribute to the emperor was also paid in the different products made from the Maguey cactus plant. Its sap was used to sweeten food, or allowed to ferment into a strong beer called *pulque*. Its thorny spines were used as sewing needles, or in drawing blood for religious ceremonies. Its fibers were twisted into ropes or fishing nets, or woven to make a coarse cloth which ordinary people wore rough against the skin. Our Lady would choose the people's most common cloth on which to impress her image. The fabric of Juan Diego's cloak or *tilma*, was made from the fibers of a plant. (Many experts believe that the tilma was made from cactus fiber. Others think it was made from palm fiber.)

The Aztec class system was very strict. If one of the common people happened to obtain a luxury item, he or she was not allowed to keep it. Instead, the person was required to give it to the local noble. The emperor received jade, turquoise and copper extracted from the remote mountain regions. He collected colorful feathers, sweet-smelling spices, and the finest cotton from the southern lowlands. Every species of shells and all kinds of pearls came from coastal tribes. From everywhere, the emperor could expect piles of lush jaguar skins, richly embroidered cloaks over which the women had labored for hundreds of hours, and rare handmade papers destined to become the books in which the scribes would draw their elaborate pictographs.

Most of the natives of that fertile and diverse land had a great respect for the position of the nobles, and most especially of the emperor, the empress, and their children. Because of this, the form in which the Blessed Mother, expectant with her holy Child, would come to them would fill them with reverential awe and respect. The manner of her coming would be so perfectly adapted to the ways of both the ancient tribes and the European Spaniards that both would immediately understand her place in God's plan. Mary's coming would bring an end to the cruelty of the old rule and liberate the oppressed Indian tribes, giving them the freedom to choose life, and to worship the only One worthy of worship: the one, holy, true God of love.

Emperor Montezuma was a tyrant who ruled his people without mercy. He held immense wealth and controlled armies of loyal warriors who had been taught in school that it was an honor to die for him. The Aztec educational system kept the social classes rigidly fixed. Only boys attended school, yet even within their ranks, favoritism was practiced.

For the peasant boys, who were considered "beneath" the noble class, studies included no reading or writing, but only the fighting arts, military discipline, and a verbal "catechism" of their religion. While rich, noble boys studied these, too, they were also privileged to be taught reading and writing, law, mathematics, government, and architecture.

Regularly, the great war drum in the center of the city beat out its cry of death. It was sounded not because another tribe was threatening the Aztecs, but because the Aztec priests had need of human blood. When the supply of prisoners grew low, the pagan priests, fearing being caught without enough blood to appease the gods, put out the call for human victims.

All males over fifteen dropped what they were doing and donned head-to-toe "armor." This armor was made of cotton that had been soaked again and again in salt water and dried until it was stiff. As the boys and men rushed to assemble for a raid, they grabbed ornate shields of wood and leather, bows and arrows, slings, battle axes, spears and their dreaded *maquahuitl* (mah-KWAH-weet), which were wooden clubs spiked with flakes of glassy, razor sharp obsidian, a volcanic rock.

The Aztec males had been trained, from the time they first attended school, to use these fearsome weapons mercilessly. According to their beliefs, war was absolutely necessary, for the gods had an unquenchable "need" for blood. The sun god, for instance, would not rise unless he was fed human blood, and nothing made *Tlaloc*, the god of rain, more willing to send showers than the sacrifice of a crying baby. Since tears resembled rain, the god, seeing a crying baby, might be reminded that the Aztec fields needed to be watered right about then.

Although the Aztecs killed, on the spot, anyone who opposed their aims, they had a deliberate policy of trying not to destroy their victims in battle. Their goal was to capture as many as possible alive by either disarming them or wounding them. They were to take these terrified captives into their city, where they would be properly sacrificed, still alive, to their gods. The prisoners had no hope of escape while they awaited their terrible fate. If any of their tribesmen attempted to save them, the Aztecs would either capture the would-be rescuers, or kill them too. The main goal of the Aztec war was simply to acquire the blood needed to please their gods.

Aztec warriors were paid in rich and showy clothes for their displays of bravery. If they showed special cruelty, they were even awarded slaves from among their captives.

Emperor Montezuma never forgot his sister's dream. He counted it in with the Aztec belief that the world had been destroyed and recreated four times in the past and that their own world was the fifth—and final—for their people. Astrologers and Aztec priests preached, "The next time our empire falls, it will never arise again."

Montezuma looked to the skies for special signs. At the time of Hernando Cortes' arrival, the stars were set just right for the prophecies to be fulfilled. At the end of each fifty-two-year cycle dictated by their calendars, the Mexican peoples expected the end of the world. An *Acatl*—or end-year occurred just before 1519. In that year, there were eclipses of the sun and the moon, and a comet with a huge fiery tail had sped through the sky.

One day, his tight network of overseers and spies informed Emperor Montezuma, "Hernando Cortes, the leader of the bearded Spaniards, is coming to see you." Montezuma thought that Cortes himself was the god who was supposed to take away his kingdom. Of course, he had mistaken Cortes—a creature—for his Creator, the God in whom Cortes believed.

In his great mercy, however, God would send his Blessed Mother to correct things. Mary would show herself in a way that was very familiar to the Indians, who gave so much importance to signs and symbols and who read by means of pictographs. Using the native people's own meaningful symbols, Mary would point the way to the truth in the midst of the confusion. She would show that God is greater than any of the persons or things he has created. She would come to protect a people already too much oppressed by superstition, error, and the greed of others.

## 8

# THE EMPEROR'S ERROR

Of course, Cortes was not a god but only a man. Princess Papantzin had said, "The strangers will bring *knowledge* of the true God." Montezuma's pagan beliefs were about to cause the downfall of his empire.

Cortes and only 650 men and 11 horses began the march across Mexico to Tenochtitlan. But on the way, many men from the neighboring Mexica tribes, already angry and hostile toward the Aztecs, joined him. A woman named Malinche, whom the Spaniards called Doña Marina, translated for Cortes. The band of Spaniards and native warriors swelled to an army of 5,000 before they reached the Aztec capital of Tenochtitlan.

Montezuma welcomed Cortes and his huge army of Indians into Tenochtitlan. "Yes! Yes! Readily!" the emperor responded when he was asked to become a vassal, or servant, of Cortes' Spanish king. "I promise to observe the laws of your ruler."

Cortes and his followers were overwhelmed by the city of Tenochtitlan, where 200,000 people lived in four distinct neighborhoods, each with a large open square at its center. Districts were linked by a system of walkways of pounded earth rising above the surface of the lake on which the city was built. The names of the neighborhoods gave an idea of their nature. There was "Mosquito Fen," "Heron's Home," and "Flowery Meadow." Each neighborhood had its own character, determined by that of the family-based clans who lived there. Each clan, or *Calpulli*, elected a leader, built its own temple, maintained the law of the Aztecs, and made its own tribute to the emperor.

Bernal Diaz del Castilo, a Spanish chronicler, wrote, "Montezuma's palace was so huge that even though I walked through it until I was tired, I never saw all of it. Not only did it contain vast apartments for lodging, but a courthouse, a pagan temple, offices for scribes, a library for their writings, meeting rooms so large that some of them could comfortably seat 3,000 people.

"Montezuma had separate apartments for each of his wives and her daughters. In comfort, the royal ladies passed much of their time weaving fine cloths and embroidering them with exquisite threads made not only of the finest materials, but also of spun gold, silver, and copper."

"Enchanting!" the Spaniards exclaimed as they walked through the sprawling palace gardens, smelled the exotic flowers and watched thousands of hummingbirds hovering. In the emperor's zoo they got their first look at many of the unusual creatures of this new country.

But the time for admiring the Aztecs' achievements soon ended. The problem Cortes had left behind in Cuba soon caught up with him. Diego Velasquez, his commander in Cuba, had sent 18 vessels and almost 1,000 men to punish Cortes for his disobedience. Cortes took 250 of his men and left the great city of the Aztecs, on a march to the coast. Not wanting to lose the ground he gained with Montezuma, he instructed the rest of his soldiers, "Stay here in Tenochtitlan, as guests of the emperor."

# 9

# TRAGEDY!

As they observed the daily life of the Aztecs, the young Spanish soldiers were shocked to witness the spectacle of human sacrifice. "This must stop!" they protested to Emperor Montezuma.

"These visitors are troublemakers!" the Aztec priests insisted. "Everyone knows that if we stop offering blood to the sun god, the world will end! If these Europeans enjoy daily sunshine, it is only because we are getting the sun god to rise! They should be grateful to us!"

The Spanish men, who had been chosen for Cortes' voyage because of their extraordinary courage and valor, had been raised and educated in a Christian culture. "We were born into noble families in which honor, respect for others, dignity and love reign," they told each other. "We cannot let this horror continue!"

The Spaniards were hot-tempered whenever honor was offended. "Respect is something to which every person has a right by birth, by virtue of being a child of God," they insisted. "But to act like this is to lose all claims to respect."

The Spanish soldiers became sick with outrage. "We have been taught to fight battles for causes we understand, but you make yourselves evil by this senseless spilling of innocent blood!" they told the Aztecs. "You are acting less than human!" The Spaniards decided they had to stop the massacres at any cost.

Few of the Indians who had joined the Spaniards had ever even been inside the city of Tenochtitlan. "It is the fearsome place of execution!" they exclaimed. Now that they were witnessing the sacrificial rituals, they too were beside themselves with anger. "Peace is impossible without drastic action!" they cried.

Fights broke out throughout the city, each side feeling justified in murdering the other.

The remaining 400 Spaniards and 5,000 Indians, all guests of Montezuma, vented their hatred, and the Aztecs, taught to be fierce and unforgiving, never yielded.

Meanwhile, Cortes and the soldiers who were with him staged a sneak attack by night on the 1,000 men who had been sent by Velasquez to capture him as a traitor. When these new conquistadors heard what Cortes had found in Mexico, they shifted their allegiance from Velasquez to Cortes and marched back to Tenochtitlan with him. Thousands lay dead by the time the new army arrived. The 175-year-old city was being toppled. Three-quarters of the Spanish soldiers had already been killed. Others had been taken prisoner. Those Aztecs who had been opposed to Montezuma from the beginning, and who resented his friendliness to the foreigners, took this chaotic opportunity to murder the emperor. The reign of Montezuma had come to an end.

The greatest outrage and offense to the Spaniards had also occurred. Some of the men, for whom Cortes had vowed personal responsibility to their families, had been dragged onto pagan altars and sacrificed to gods that existed only in the imaginations of their Aztec executioners. Cortes saw this horror as nothing short of offering homage to the devil. "I will destroy the city of Tenochtitlan!" he vowed.

In a fury fueled by revenge and a sense of justice, Cortes and his fresh recruits

*Tenochtitlan was being toppled.*

joined in the attack upon Tenochtitlan. They killed without mercy. They leveled the temples. They snatched up any riches they could find.

Once they had retreated to a safe place outside the city, Cortes dropped beneath an ancient cedar tree and wept. "I have conquered the Aztecs," he said, "but at what a price! Four hundred fifty of my valiant men and 4,000 of our native allies are dead!"

Cortes handed over to the care of the Franciscans those Aztecs who remained in the city. Bishop Zumarraga told his friars, "As heartsick as we are over this enormous tragedy, we must respond with generous love so that we may help heal not only our own people, but the poor Aztecs who have lost home, family, friends, and religion in one blow!"

The entire event had disgusted the Spaniards and caused further divisions among them. The Indians of Mexico, of course, were still divided. Conditions were ripe for more war, and at every turn treachery and danger lurked.

Bishop Zumarraga and the friars prayed to the Blessed Virgin Mary, "Dear Mother of God, help us!" *Will my sign ever come?* the bishop wondered. *The native people resist our teaching more and more! And who could blame them?* "Lord, do not abandon these other children of yours!" he prayed.

The bishop could not have known it, but the moment for the great miracle of the Americas had arrived!

## 10

# THE MIRACLE AT LAST

It was Saturday, December 9, 1531. In the early morning twilight, fifty-seven-year-old Juan Diego was on his way to church for a catechism lesson. His wife Maria Lucia had died two years earlier, and Juan now lived with his uncle Juan Bernardino, who had raised him. The church was almost nine miles away, but Juan was happy to make the sacrifice. He loved his Christian faith.

Soon Juan Diego came to the brooding outline of Tepeyac Hill. Before becoming a Christian, Juan had cringed with dread at having to pass this gloomy place. The Indians believed that the mother goddess, Tonantzin, who demanded the blood of babies, lived on Tepeyac. But Juan Diego now knew that she didn't exist. He wished that one day soon other members of his tribe would come to know this truth.

Suddenly, Juan heard what seemed like music. But it was the most beautiful music he could ever have imagined! It sounded as if every kind of bird had burst into song. The incredible sound surrounded Juan Diego, giving him a thrill of joy. He spun around in delight, letting the song become a part of him. *It's amazing!* Juan thought. *The birds seem to be praising God! I've never heard birds sing like this before. And it's December. It's too cold for them to be out. What's happening?* he wondered. *Am I in heaven?*

Juan was about to discover that heaven had, in fact, come down to earth. The privileged man could not have known it then, but the birds were witnessing a wondrous sight in which he would soon have a share. In a moment Juan's heart would soar, too!

Just as abruptly as it had started, the music stopped. The sound of an enchanting and motherly voice replaced it. A woman's voice was calling in Juan Diego's native *Nahuatl* (NAH-wat) language, "Juantzin!" (This was the equivalent of "Juanito" in Spanish, or something like "Johnny" in English.) "Juantzin!" the voice repeated. In the Nahuatl language adding the ending "tzin" to a person's name was a sign of special love and respect. This form of address was only used for family and close friends.

The captivating voice seemed to pen-
etrate into Juan's very heart. He felt himself
mysteriously drawn to it as he scrambled to
the top of the hill.

There Juan came face to face with a wonderful sight! Before him, shining in light,
stood the most beautiful Aztec maiden he
had ever seen! She appeared to be only
about fourteen years old, but she possessed
great majesty. The dazzling light that radi-
ated from her person was brighter than the
sun's, yet so gentle that sunlight would later
seem harsh to Juan. The astonished Indian
desired only to please the young Woman.
He could have stayed there forever, just gazing at her loveliness. The light coming from
the Lady flooded the rocks, prickly pear
bushes and mesquite plants with colors so
intense that these shone like the most precious emeralds, rubies and sapphires. Even
the thorn bushes and dried wisps of plants
appeared to be dipped in the shining gold
and delicate silver of the Lady's reflection.
Everything around the Aztec Maiden
seemed to be alive with the very life of God!
"What's happening?" Juan murmured in
amazement.

This was no ordinary person. Juan was sure of that. The young Lady's star-studded mantle was decorated with designs worn by Aztec queens. Her compassionate face commanded instant respect, making Juan yearn to become her servant. She was certainly someone very special and very great! Although very young, the Lady's face beamed a motherly love so gracious, so good, and so powerful that it made Juan Diego feel safe from every danger. He sank to his knees and waited for her to speak.

"Juantzin, my little son," the Lady said, "where are you going?"

"My Holy One, my Lady, I am on my way to your house at Tlatelolco!" Juan Diego answered. "I am going to learn the holy things which our priests teach us."

The already radiant Lady smiled, and Juan's heart swelled at her approval. She nodded. "You must know, and be certain, littlest of my sons," she said, "that I am truly the perfect and ever-Virgin Mary, holy Mother of the true God, through whose favor we live, the Creator, Lord of Heaven and Earth."

The beautiful Lady continued, "I wish very much that my church be built here.

Here I will show all my love, my mercy, my help and my protection. I am truly your merciful Mother—a mother to you and to all the other people dear to me who call upon me, who search for me, who trust in me.

"I am the Mother of all who live united in this land, and of all people, of all who are devoted to me, and of those who come to me for help.

"Here I will hear their weeping and their sorrows, and I will cure them and make things better for them.

"Go to the house of the Bishop of Mexico City and tell him that I sent you and that it is my desire to have a church built here. Tell him all that you have seen and heard.

"Now, my son, you have heard my wish. Go in peace and be sure that I will repay you for doing what I ask."

Juan bowed to the ground. "My Holy One, my Lady," he whispered, "I go to carry out your command as your humble servant. Wait a little while for me."

Getting quickly to his feet, Juan Diego hurried off to Mexico City, which had been built on the ruins of Tenochtitlan. As the sun rose, he followed the route of the dike that led to the city.

Juan had promised the Mother of God that he would bring her message to the bishop. And he was determined to keep his promise!

## 11

# MARY'S SECOND AND
# THIRD VISITS

Juan Diego found Bishop Zumarraga's house. After a long wait, he was finally admitted. Juan told the learned and holy man everything, through an interpreter. The bishop asked many questions. A wonderful excitement began to rise in his heart. *But in matters like these, one must proceed carefully,* Bishop Zumarraga reminded himself. *What if the man has only imagined all this, or what if it is a trick of the devil, who seems especially ruthless and busy these days?*

The bishop sat silently stroking his beard. *If God's Mother is truly appearing and asking for a church to be built,* his thoughts continued, *it will come about in spite of my own doubts. I will wait and see what happens.*

Bishop Zumarraga rose. "Thank you for sharing your story, Juan," he said kindly. "You may go now. We can speak about these things another time."

Juan rushed back to Tepeyac Hill. He felt certain that Mary would be waiting for him.

He was right! His heart pounding with joy, he scaled the rocky hill. There was the young Lady, in that same wonderful light. Juan sank to his knees.

"My very dear Daughter!" he began, not sure how to address the young Maiden who had called him her son. "My Queen, my Lady Most High, I did what you asked. Even though I had to wait a long time, I did get to see the bishop. I gave him your message. He listened quietly to me and asked me questions. But I don't think he believed me, because he told me to come back again, so that he could examine the matter further. He thinks that the church you are asking for is my idea, not yours. Please, my Lady, send some important person to bring your message to the bishop—someone the bishop will respect and believe. I am only a poor, humble villager. Pardon me, my Queen. I hope I have not displeased you."

The Lady smiled at Juan Diego with so much love. What he said was true: he was a simple man, good and sincere. That was why she had chosen him to deliver her message. "Listen, my well-beloved son," she told him, "I have many others whom I could send to the bishop if I wished, but I want to send you. Tomorrow I want you to go back to the bishop and tell him to build me the church that I ask for. Tell him that she who sends you is the Virgin Mary, the Mother of God."

Looking at her brilliant face, Juan Diego felt encouraged. "I hope I didn't displease you by what I said, my Queen and my Lady," he quietly repeated. "I will be happy to go and see the bishop again. I will do everything that you ask. I just thought that the bishop might be more willing to listen to someone more important than I." The Mother of God smiled understandingly. "Wait for me here, my Lady," Juan added. "Tomorrow, at the setting of the sun, I will bring back to you the bishop's answer. I leave you in peace, my exalted Daughter. God keep you."

Before dawn the next morning, Juan Diego hurried to Mass in Mexico City. Then he presented himself at the bishop's house. Again the servants kept him waiting for hours before letting him in.

Juan pleaded with Bishop Zumarraga. He even cried. The bishop rested his hand on Juan's shoulder. "Be calm, my son," he urged. The bishop then asked Juan many questions, over and over again. He was impressed with Juan's goodness. Juan seemed to really be telling the truth. But still, Bishop Zumarraga did not act. Instead, he gave Juan another mission: "Go back and ask the Lady for a sign."

What happened next was a miracle in itself. The bishop instructed his servants, "Follow Juan Diego. Watch where he goes and to whom he speaks." Bishop Zumarraga realized that as the spiritual leader of the Church in Mexico, it was his duty to find out the truth. He had to be sure that Juan Diego was neither lying nor imagining things.

The servants followed Juan all the way back to Tepeyac Hill. Then, right before their eyes, Juan vanished! The men searched, but could not find him. They returned to the bishop's house, denouncing Juan Diego. "He's a fraud, or maybe even a sorcerer!" They were willing to swear he had truly "disappeared"! *What power could have accomplished this?* the bishop wondered.

Actually, Bishop Zumarraga's servants had walked very close to Juan Diego, but God had not allowed them to see him. Mary had hidden him in her light, and even hidden the light itself!

Juan quickly told the Blessed Virgin all about his audience with Bishop Zumarraga.

"So be it, my son," she answered. "Return here tomorrow and I will give you the sign the bishop has asked for. Once you have it, he will believe you. Remember that I will reward you for everything you have suffered. Go now. I will be waiting for you tomorrow."

## 12

# THE SIGN

That night, Juan Diego's uncle, Juan Bernardino, contracted a terrible fever. As the hours dragged on, it only worsened. "Everyone who has caught this illness has died!" Juan Diego's neighbors warned him.

By morning, Juan could see that his uncle was dying. Among the Indians, the authority of an uncle was the same as that of a parent. And Juan Diego especially loved this uncle who had raised him. "Please ...Juan...bring me a priest..." the old man gasped. "I wish...to receive...the...sacraments."

Juan rushed out of the house. *As much as it pains me,* he thought, *I have to avoid the path where I've been seeing the Blessed Virgin Mary. I can't stop to see her now!* Juan skirted around Tepeyac Hill by another route.

*"Juantzin!"* (HWAN-tzin) he suddenly heard. *"Juantzin!"* Juan cringed in embarrassment. Wrapped in light, the Mother of God was descending from the top of the hill. "Where are you going, my little son? And

what road is this you are taking?" she asked with an understanding smile.

Juan had been caught. He didn't know what to say, so he tried to make small talk. "My beloved Daughter, and my Lady, God keep you! Did you sleep well? How are you feeling today?" But looking into those beautiful eyes that saw all, Juan quickly changed his tone. "Please don't be angry with what I have to say," he continued. "My uncle, a servant of yours, is dying. I'm hurrying to call a priest for him. As soon as I've done this, I will come back to see you. Forgive me, my Lady," he pleaded. "Have patience with me. I promise that I will come back to see you tomorrow."

Mary listened serenely. Then, with more compassion than ever, she said, "Listen, my son, to what I tell you now. Do not be troubled, or disturbed by anything. Do not be afraid of illness, or suffering, or pain. Don't you know that I will protect you? Don't you remember that I am your Mother? Do you need anything else? Don't worry. Your uncle is already cured."

Juan Diego experienced a great feeling of relief. He was sure that what our Lady said was true. "Then I will go on your errand right now," he eagerly replied.

"Go, my son, to the top of the hill where you first saw me. There you will find many flowers. Gather them and bring them to me."

Even though it was December and very cold, even though no flowers grew on that barren hill, and even though he had been there only the day before and had not seen any flowers, Juan did not doubt the Blessed Mother's word. He climbed the bleak hill. When he reached the top, he gasped in amazement. He was surrounded by the most beautiful flowers he had ever seen, their perfect petals trembling in the breeze that comes with the sunrise. Such roses, and in every color! With each breath, Juan drew in their heavenly fragrance. As he stooped to pluck each rose, he was struck by its perfection and loveliness.

In the ancient style of country people who use aprons, hats or shoes for carrying things, Juan Diego made a "basket" of his cloak, his tilma, tucking the delicate blossoms into its hollow.

He excitedly carried the flowers to Mary. The Mother of God then rearranged them with her own hands! "My little son," she said as she worked, "these roses are the sign which you are to take to the bishop. Tell

*"Take these roses to the bishop."*

him, in my name, that he must do what I ask." Our Lady looked into Juan's eyes and smiled. "You will be my ambassador. I trust you. Don't show what you are carrying to anyone but the bishop. Tell him everything. Say that I ordered you to go to the top of the hill and that you found these roses there. Explain everything so that the bishop will give his help and the church I ask for may be built."

Juan didn't want to leave Mary, but now that he had the sign, the proof that she had really appeared to him, he was anxious to see the bishop. He hurried off to Mexico City, his heart throbbing with excitement.

The doorkeepers at the bishop's gate were getting annoyed. "When will he stop pestering the bishop?" one grumbled when he saw Juan coming up the path. "You can't go in," they told Juan roughly. But when they saw that he was carrying something, the Spaniards insisted on taking a peek. Afraid that the men would send him away, Juan showed them a few of the flowers. They gasped at the sight of the Castilian roses. They had not seen these since they'd left their homeland! The doorkeepers reached into Juan's tilma, trying to seize the roses, but their hands passed right through the flowers, as if through air! Bewildered, they rushed Juan Diego in to the bishop.

"I have the Lady's sign!" Juan announced. He dropped the corners of his tilma and the miraculous flowers tumbled to the floor. The bishop stared, and then, overcome with awe, fell to his knees. Juan saw that Bishop Zumarraga was no longer looking at the roses. His tearful eyes were fixed on Juan Diego's tilma. Looking down, Juan was astounded to see that there, in brilliant colors, was a magnificent picture of the Blessed Virgin Mary, just as she had appeared on Tepeyac Hill!

With trembling hands, Bishop Zumarraga untied Juan Diego's tilma. He reverently carried it to his private chapel. *The most fitting company for a portrait made by heaven*, he thought, *is Jesus himself, in the Blessed Sacrament*. The bishop and the other members of his household knelt in the presence of the image and praised God for the gift of his Mother.

Bishop Zumarraga wanted Juan Diego to tell him every detail of the Lady's appearance that day. Juan slept at the bishop's house that night as an honored guest. The next day many people accompanied Juan and the bishop to the places where Mary had stood on Tepeyac Hill. The hilltop was brown and bare. There was not even a trace of a flower to be seen.

From the hill, Juan went to check on his uncle at their house in Tulpetlac. He found the villagers rejoicing. "While you were gone to get me a priest," the old man told his nephew, "the Blessed Virgin Mary appeared to me. She cured me instantly! She wants a church built where you saw her. She said that the bishop would call her by the name the 'ever-Virgin Holy Mary of Guadalupe.'"

The news that Mexico had received visits from the great Mother of God spread like wildfire.

"If we work day and night to build a chapel in our Lady's honor," the people decided, "the bishop can place her image in it during the Christmas season!"

On the day after Christmas, a lively procession carried Juan Diego's tilma from the bishop's chapel to the new adobe shrine on the hill. Along the way, people laid fragrant herbs before the feet of those who carried the image. They built arbors under which the picture of the Mother of God would pass. Dressed in their best hand-woven, colorful costumes, the native people honored Mary with music, dancing, and singing.

As part of the celebration, the Indians even staged mock battles. In all the excitement, one man was accidentally shot through the neck with an arrow. He fell lifeless at the feet of his friends. A shout went up that demonstrated the people's confidence in our Lady: "Bring him before the tilma! Bring him before the tilma!" As soon as the Indians laid the dead man in front of Mary's image, he got to his feet! This miracle brought hope and joy both to the oppressed Indians and the weary Spaniards. How fitting it was that Mary, who had given birth to Jesus, the Life of the world, should raise one of her children to life through Jesus' power during the Christmas celebrations! The troubled inhabitants of the New World had truly found a compassionate mother in Our Lady of Guadalupe! She was their helper, their friend, their intercessor before the one true God!

"May I appoint you custodian of the new shrine?" the bishop soon asked Juan Diego.

"I would be most honored, Your Excellency," Juan replied. Juan and his wife Maria Lucia had never had any children. After Maria Lucia's death Juan had centered his life more and more on God. He was happy now to think that he would live at the shrine where he could spend more time in prayer and help visitors come closer to God and the Virgin Mary.

"It will mean telling the story of the events of the Blessed Mother's apparitions over and over, to everyone who comes there," the bishop explained.

"I will never tire of telling it!" replied Juan Diego. "I will tell it with joy until the day I die!"

"Good!" the bishop nodded, smiling. "We will build you a small house by the chapel."

Soon many of the native people wanted to know more about the Blessed Mother's visits to Juan Diego. It was Don Antonio Valeriano, a distant relative of Emperor Montezuma, who wrote the Nahuatl language account of the apparitions. It was called *"Nican Mopohua"* (NEE-kan mo-POH-wah).

The Indians, who used to fear the terrible and greedy pagan goddess, now came in peace to Tepeyac Hill. They witnessed countless miracles as proofs of our Lady's love. A steady stream of pilgrims came at every hour, on foot, to honor the holy image and to hear the details of Mary's apparitions. Many of the native people experienced personal conversions from their old beliefs, and asked to be taught about Catholicism. Artists even painted the story of the apparitions of the Lady to Juan Diego. Their paintings were circulated among the people as visual storybooks.

Juan Diego, whose humility and love of God had been an inspiration to the other converts even before the apparitions, became a living witness of the mercy of God toward all his people. Without ever boasting about the favors our Lady had granted him, Juan simply told the story of her apparitions to anyone who wanted to hear it. He gave God all the honor for these wonderful events and never took any credit for himself.

Juan, Mary's special servant, was the sacristan of the shrine at Tepeyac for about seventeen years. He was always ready to help the chaplain with whatever work had to be done. Juan finally died of the plague in 1548. He was seventy-four years old.

Juan Diego was buried in the chapel of Our Lady of Guadalupe, next to his uncle, who had passed away four years before him. Four months after Juan Diego's death, Bishop Zumarraga died. Over the years Juan's remains were transferred from one chapel to another, accompanying Our Lady of Guadalupe's image as it was moved. After 1649, however, no one recorded the location of his grave. Today we still do not know where Juan Diego is buried.

Witnesses who were questioned after Juan Diego died all agreed that he was a saint. They spoke about his great humility, love of neighbor and love of prayer. They told about his penances, his fasting, and his strong devotion to Jesus in the Holy Eucharist. During Juan's time, it was the custom to receive Holy Communion only once a week. But the bishop gave Juan Diego special permission to receive Communion three times a week. Juan used to spend quiet time thanking God for the many blessings he had received. He offered the Lord the gift of his grateful heart.

## 14

# HIDDEN MESSAGES

For a while, the most amazing aspect of the image of Our Lady of Guadalupe on Juan Diego's tilma remained hidden from the Spaniards. They didn't recognize that there were wonderful messages concealed in the picture itself. The Indians, however, accustomed to reading signs and symbols, saw that deep meanings lay in the details of the image of Our Lady of Guadalupe.

Many Indians—both Christians and non-Christians—came to the Tepeyac Hill shrine to study this image that had come from heaven. The most learned Indian scholars discussed it, and the peasants noticed mysterious messages in it. "Who is this Lady?" they all wanted to know.

"Her mantle is colored with the blue-green dye reserved for Aztec royalty," they remarked. "She wears a golden dress edged with the most delicate fur. Her clothes are embroidered with costly gold. And look! They have been stitched by the most masterly craftsman! She must be a very powerful queen, for only the highest noble is allowed to dress in this manner!"

The stars that adorned Mary's mantle were arranged exactly as they were in the night sky. Halley's Comet had been overhead at the dawn of that morning on which the Queen of the Universe told her servant Juan to pick the flowers on the once-barren hill. If Aztecs gazing at the sky that day took this as a sign that some great event was occurring, they were right.

"The Lady wears the stars for her decoration," the natives of Mexico told each other. The eight-pointed stars signify regeneration in the Indian tradition. "She must surely be greater than the gods of the skies. And count the stars. There are forty-six—the exact number of constellations visible in the skies on December 12, the night of her last apparition! If she has knowledge enough to paint with just the right number of stars, she must be greater, even, than the very *study* of the stars!"

"And could she be greater than the mysterious and beautiful moon god? Look! She stands on the moon, dimming it until it is black. It is left without power!"

*So must we now honor her as the new mother goddess?* the non-Christian Indians wondered. *Is she the god whose image we must place in our empty shrine? Is she "the true god, the one through whom everything lives"?*

"Look closely at her humble face," they told each other. "She bows her head in prayer."

"Her hands are folded quietly," they added, "yet they are ready to act, like a servant whose talents are at someone else's disposal. She is not a goddess at all. She is worshiping someone else."

"But who is that someone?" they asked as they looked for signs. They found two. "The Lady's gold dress is tied with a sash. That means she is expecting a baby." This was an honored condition among the Aztecs.

"She was housed in this shrine during the Christmas season," the converts among them observed, "the time when we celebrate the birth of Jesus. During Christmas, here in what the Europeans call the New World, she gave birth to her Son in a new way."

"She's looking down," everyone noticed, "toward her child. Perhaps we should all be worshipping him!"

"Maybe," others insisted, "but she is also looking down at that symbol at her neck."

"Look well! She is revering both her child and the symbol," they decided.

"And this symbol rests over the place from which the voice comes. She wants to speak to us through means of this symbol."

And what was this symbol? It was the cross on the Spaniards' banners, the very cross Princess Papantzin had seen in her dream years before!

"The Lady's child died on the cross," explained the Indians who had heard the preaching of the Franciscan friars. "Even though she isn't a goddess, this Lady is greater than the greatest god we used to worship," they exclaimed. "Those gods do not exist, and this Lady who once walked the earth as we do, now lives in eternity, with her Son, the true God! We are her children, and she is here to help us find our way to heaven."

The native people also saw the rays of the sun behind the Lady, conforming its own ageless shape to her petite outline. "This means she is greater than the sun god," the non-Christians said.

"In fact," the Indian converts noted, "the sun continues to shine even as we honor her one God without human sacrifice. See? She only eclipses the sun. It is still visible behind her!"

People began flocking to the Franciscan priests. "Tell us more about your religion!" they begged. Soon many millions of New World residents eagerly embraced baptism. "Their numbers exceed that of the Catholics who have left the Church because of the confusion in Europe," the bishop noted in amazement.

"We Europeans may have heard the good news about Jesus first," the priests said, "but that doesn't guarantee that we will practice our religion better. Many of these converts put the European colonists to shame! See how well they incorporate Jesus' teachings into their lives and traditions."

Through "Holy Mary, the painted girl," the worlds of the Spaniards and the native peoples finally blended in peace. The Blessed Virgin had become the true patroness of the new land called the Americas.

## 15

# OUR LADY'S TITLE

Juan Diego's uncle, Juan Bernardino, spoke the Nahuatl language. When he repeated the title by which our Lady had identified herself to him, it sounded like "Guadalupe" to the Spaniards. In fact, "Our Lady of Guadalupe" has been the title by which Mary, as she appeared to Juan Diego, has become known and loved.

There is still some doubt, however, that Mary actually called herself "Guadalupe." Some scholars believe she used the Nahuatl word, *"Coatlaxopeuh,"* (KOAH-tlash-oh-PEU-u) since neither the letters "g" nor "d" exist in Nahuatl. In religious instruction classes, the Franciscan friars had long before pointed out to the Indians the passage from Genesis in the Bible, in which God the Father promises to send a woman whose Son would crush the head of the evil serpent. The Indian name Coatlaxopeuh means precisely that, *"she who breaks, stamps and crushes the serpent."* This interpretation of the name by which our Lady called herself seems to make sense, because her apparitions in Mexico did succeed in ending the worship of the false gods, the chief of which was a serpent.

Perhaps it pleases God to let Mary's title remain a mystery to us. Of course, God can make it possible for the Blessed Mother to speak any language. We know that Mary spoke the Nahuatl language perfectly when she appeared to Juan Diego. She even used the Nahuatl practice of beginning with a less important idea and building up to a more important one in order to communicate an abstract concept. For example, Mary first told Juan Diego, "It is I." Then she went on to give him one of her titles, "The Virgin Mary." Finally, she revealed to him her greatest identity, "The Mother of God".

When the Spanish interpreter, who was born in the Extremadura region of Spain, first heard Uncle Juan Bernardino say the name by which our Lady identified herself, he might have naturally imagined "Guadalupe." In the Extremadura, there exists a shrine dedicated to Mary. It is called the shrine of Guadalupe. In the 1400s, decades before Cortes sailed from Spain, priests (belonging to the same Franciscan order that would later travel to the New World) placed a statue of the Blessed Mother there. Except for the fact that Mary is carrying her Son Jesus in her arms, this statue is amazingly similar to the image of Mary on Juan Diego's tilma. The statue in Extremadura wears a star-studded mantle. It is standing on a crescent moon. A small angel is holding Mary up. Even the sun's rays jut out behind the Blessed Mother just as they do in the tilma image.

We can't help wondering about the connection between this Spanish shrine and the New World. Christopher Columbus, who had had our Lady's initials interwoven into his signature because of his devotion to her, not only prayed at the Extremadura shrine, but also requested that he be buried there. Just at the time when Columbus was outfitting *La Niña, La Pinta* and *La Santa Maria*, Queen Isabella and King Ferdinand of Spain, who sponsored his voyage, were making a two-week retreat at that very same shrine!

The hourly ship's logs that Columbus kept have been preserved and still exist. They give us an accurate and detailed account of his expedition. They tell us that every half hour, the entire crew prayed aloud on each of Columbus's three ships. As was the custom of European sailors at that time, Columbus's crew also sang the *Hail, Holy Queen* every evening at sunset. As the men hoisted sails, their sea chanteys were litanies to the saints. In the privacy of his captain's quarters, Columbus himself prayed from his breviary three times a day.

Our Lady showed her motherly protection during the voyagers' worst moments. One time, when a strange lack of wind left the ships stalled in eerie stillness, the fearful crew was on the verge of mutiny. Columbus sharply reprimanded his men for their lack of faith, and began praying to Mary. One by one, the sailors joined in his prayer. As their voices echoed off those mysterious waters, a west wind suddenly rose up, billowing the ships' sails and thrusting them forward. The men felt confident again.

The very next day, the unusual calm returned. Again the three ships were stranded. Again the crew felt that something terrible was going to happen to them. Again Columbus scolded his men and began praying to the Blessed Mother. Suddenly, a swell lifted the boats. A gust of wind pressed them westward. Rough seas rolled under them, propelling them so speedily toward the shores of the New World that Columbus compared the strange events to Moses' leading the Israelites out of the captivity of Egypt. In his captain's log, he described the incident as a "miracle."

During their most terrifying storm at sea, when *La Niña* was in danger of sinking into the dark depths of the pounding ocean, Columbus and his men begged our Lady to save them. Columbus made a vow to her then. If she would save *La Niña*, he would make a pilgrimage, barefoot and in sackcloth. Where did he promise to go? To the Spanish shrine of Guadalupe! Columbus kept that promise when he returned to Spain. When we consider that there are so many different shrines to our Lady in Spain and that Columbus was Italian and not Spanish, we can't help but wonder why he chose the Guadalupe shrine in Extremadura. What did this shrine have to do with the settling of the American continents? When we add that Mary's American apparition was named for Guadalupe, we are really filled with wonder!

Hernando Cortes himself was born in the Extremadura region of Spain. Before his fateful trip to the New World, he also made a pilgrimage to the famous Guadalupe shrine to ask for our Lady's protection. So did Bishop Juan Zumarraga before he left Spain to travel to the New World. It seems that God was trying to show that just as Mary has always interceded with him for the needs of the people of the Old Word, so she would for the people of the New World.

At Tepeyac Hill God sent his Mother in a most wonderful way to all the people of the Americas so that she could lead them all to him!

# 16

# SCIENCE PROVES THE MIRACLE

Even today, after almost 500 years, the cloth of Juan Diego's tilma, woven from coarse plant fibers, shows no signs of decay. No other cactus or palm fiber cloths exist from Juan Diego's time because they naturally fall apart after about twenty years! The colors of the picture of Mary have not faded. They are still bright and clear. In 1936, the German Nobel Prize winner in Chemistry, Richard Kuhn, examined some fibers from the tilma. What he discovered astonished the world. There is no coloring of any kind in the fabric. The color of Mary's image on the tilma hasn't penetrated the threads of the actual cloth. This proves that the picture was not painted onto the cloth. Besides that, the materials used to produce what resembles colors are unknown to science.

Millions of people have touched and kissed the tilma, and hardly one of them left without lighting a votive candle to burn beneath it. For centuries, the tilma with its image was also exposed to damp stone, dust, and wind. In 1921, a bomb even exploded right in front of it. But, after all this, the tilma remains undamaged and as new looking as ever.

Our Lady's image contains an even more astonishing proof that it is authentic. In 1929, a professional photographer named Alfonso Gonzales was enlarging some photographs of the tilma. He looked closely at the Lady's eyes. To his great amazement, he found reflections of people's faces there!

In 1951, J. Carlos Salinas Chavaz was using a magnifying glass to examine a photograph of the sacred image's face. As the lens moved across the Lady's right eye, Carlos was astonished to see a man staring back at him.

A few years later, Luis Maria Martinez, then the bishop of Mexico City, asked a group of distinguished scientists to examine Mary's eyes as they appear on the tilma. On December 11, 1955, the news was made public: the scientists had indeed found reflections of people in her eyes.

Many eye doctors and scientists have greatly magnified the image of our Lady's eyes on the tilma in order to study them more closely. And they have made some astonishing discoveries. When they use the instrument an eye doctor uses to look into a patient's eyes, they can actually look into the eyes of the picture of Our Lady of Guadalupe and see the same eye structure they find in a living person's eyes.

Experts have also found that the reflections in Mary's eyes on the tilma are formed in exactly the same way they would be in a living person's eyes, at precisely the correct angles, proportions, and distortions. Researchers have compared the people reflected in the eyes of Mary's image to paintings made by artists in Juan Diego's time. They have confirmed that all four men reflected in the Lady's eyes were actually present in the room, in 1531, when Juan Diego gave Bishop Zumarraga the flowers from the Blessed Virgin. The largest face visible in Mary's eyes has been identified as none other than Juan Diego himself.

No matter what the temperature of the Basilica of Our Lady of Guadalupe, where Juan Diego's tilma is now kept, the custodians there have found that the tilma remains a constant 98.6 degrees, Fahrenheit—the temperature of a healthy human body.

Our Blessed Mother kept the promises she made to Juan Diego, and she continues to offer life and hope to her children all over

*Mary's image now hangs in her great basilica.*

the world. Mary's image, enclosed behind glass in a special frame, now hangs over the main altar of the great Basilica of Our Lady of Guadalupe, not far from Tepeyac Hill in Mexico. Today this basilica is the most popular Marian shrine in the world. Between fifteen to twenty *million* people visit it every year.

Juan Diego was beatified in Mexico by Pope John Paul II on May 6, 1990. He was canonized—declared a saint—by Pope John Paul II in Mexico on July 31, 2002. The miracle that led to his canonization took place in Mexico City in May of 1990. A troubled young man named Juan Jose Esperanza had suffered very severe head injuries after having jumped from the balcony of his home. He fell three stories to the street below. To the amazement of all the doctors, who told Mrs. Esperanza that her son was not going to live, Juan Jose quickly and completely recovered! Mrs. Esperanza had begged Juan Diego to intercede with God to save her son as he was falling to the ground.

We celebrate the memorial of Saint Juan Diego every year on December 9, the date on which Mary first appeared to him.

We celebrate the feast of Our Lady of Guadalupe each year on December 12. This is the anniversary of the date on which Mary cured Juan Diego's uncle.

Holy Mary of Guadalupe, our good Mother, bring us all to Jesus.

Saint Juan Diego, pray for us.

# PRAYER

*Thank you, Mary, for having visited Mexico so many years ago. Because of that visit you are the Patroness of the Americas, and we give you the title Our Lady of Guadalupe.*

*I know that the messages you gave Saint Juan Diego are also for all of us, your children. Help me not to be sad or disturbed by anything. Help me not to be afraid, even when bad things happen. You have told us that you are our Mother. You have promised that you will protect us. I know that you always pray to God for us.*

*Saint Juan, I want to love Jesus and Mary as you did. Ask God to make my faith strong. Help me to imitate you. I want to be always ready to do what God wants. Pray for me, Saint Juan. Amen.*

# GLOSSARY

1. **Apparition**—someone or something that appears and is able to be seen by a another person.

2. **Beatify**—the act by which the Pope, in the name of the Catholic Church, declares that a person lived a life of Gospel holiness in a heroic way. This is done after the person's life and holiness have been carefully researched. In most cases, a proven **miracle** obtained through the holy person's prayers to God is also required. The ceremony in which a person is beatified is called a *beatification*. Beatification is the second step in the process of naming a person a saint. A person who has been beatified is given the title "Blessed."

3. **Breviary**—the prayer book containing the Liturgy of the Hours, which is the public and official common prayer of the Catholic Church. Priests and religious brothers and sisters pray the Liturgy of the Hours every day. Many lay people also use this form of prayer, which is based on the Psalms.

4. **Chantey**—a song sung by sailors as they work.

5. **Chaplain**—a priest who ministers to a certain group of people.

6. **Friar**—a word meaning "brother." This is the name given to male members (both priests and brothers) of certain religious Orders, such as the Franciscans and Dominicans. While a monk works and prays inside his monastery, a friar usually ministers to God's people outside the monastery.

7. **Grace**—a participation in the life of God. Jesus won grace for us by his death on the cross.

8. **Heresy**—a denial of a truth of the Catholic faith.

9. **Hieroglyphics**—pictures or symbols that were used to represent words, syllables or sounds by some ancient civilizations.

10. **Humility**—the virtue by which we realize that everything good in us is a gift from God.

11. **Immaculate Conception**—the privilege God gave Mary in preserving her from sin from the very beginning of her existence, since she was to become the Mother of his Son. We celebrate the mystery of Mary's Immaculate Conception every year on December 8.

12. **Intercede**—(as it is used in this book) to make a request of someone for the good of another person.

13. **Miracle**—a wonderful happening which goes beyond the powers of nature and is produced by God to teach us some truth or to testify to the holiness of a person.

14. **Mutiny**—a rebellion of soldiers or sailors against their commanding officers.

15. **Pilgrims**—persons who travel to a holy place to pray and to feel closer to God. The journey they make is called a **pilgrimage.**

16. **Plague**—a deadly, highly contagious disease.

17. **Procession**—a religious event in which people walk together from one place to another in order to publicly honor God, the Blessed Virgin or the saints.

18. **Retreat**—a special time set aside for silence and deeper prayer.

19. **Sacristan**—a person who takes care of the sacred vessels, vestments and various articles used for the celebration of Mass and other liturgical services.

20. **Sackcloth**—a rough cloth worn as a sign of sorrow for one's sins, or as a sign of mourning.

21. **Ship's log**—a daily record book in which things like the ship's speed and position are kept track of.

22. **Vow**—an important promise made freely to God.

# Who are the Daughters of St. Paul?

We are Catholic sisters with a mission. Our task is to bring the love of Jesus to everyone like Saint Paul did. You can find us in over 50 countries. Our founder, Blessed James Alberione, showed us how to reach out to the world through the media. That's why we publish books, make movies and apps, record music, broadcast on radio, perform concerts, help people at our bookstores, visit parishes, host JClub book fairs, use social media and the Internet, and pray for all of you.

**Visit our Web site at www.pauline.org**

## BOOKS & MEDIA

The Daughters of St. Paul operate book and media centers at the following addresses. Visit, call or write the one nearest you today, or find us at www.paulinestore.org.

**CALIFORNIA**
3908 Sepulveda Blvd, Culver City, CA 90230          310-397-8676
3250 Middlefield Road, Menlo Park, CA 94025          650-369-4230

**FLORIDA**
145 S.W. 107th Avenue, Miami, FL 33174          305-559-6715

**HAWAII**
1143 Bishop Street, Honolulu, HI 96813          808-521-2731

**ILLINOIS**
172 North Michigan Avenue, Chicago, IL 60601          312-346-4228

**LOUISIANA**
4403 Veterans Memorial Blvd, Metairie, LA 70006          504-887-7631

**MASSACHUSETTS**
885 Providence Hwy, Dedham, MA 02026          781-326-5385

**MISSOURI**
9804 Watson Road, St. Louis, MO 63126          314-965-3512

**NEW YORK**
64 W. 38th Street, New York, NY 10018          212-754-1110

**SOUTH CAROLINA**
243 King Street, Charleston, SC 29401          843-577-0175

**TEXAS**
Currently no book center; for parish exhibits or outreach evangelization, contact: 210-569-0500, or SanAntonio@paulinemedia.com, or P.O. Box 761416,
San Antonio, TX 78245

**VIRGINIA**
1025 King Street, Alexandria, VA 22314          703-549-3806

**CANADA**
3022 Dufferin Street, Toronto, ON M6B 3T5          416-781-9131

¡También somos su fuente
para libros, videos y música en español!